Two Dimensional Christianity

Dr. Murl Edward Gwynn

Published by MEG Enterprises Publications
PO Box 2165
Reidsville, GA 30453
(912) 557-6507
murlgwynn@gmail.com
www.murlgwynn.com

Printed in the U.S.A

International Standard Book Number:
978-0-9862596-3-0

Also by Dr. Gwynn

Fighting from Victory

The gods Among Us

Chrislam – What Communion Hath Light
With Darkness?

Conflict – Christianity's Love vs. Islam's
Submission

The President Was a Good Man (A Novel)

Anything for Acceptance

Healing – The Children's Bread

Created to Live!

Easter – Not what you think!

Bless and Curse Not!

To the third and fourth Generation!

ACKNOWLEDGMENTS

Ruth, my wife and best friend!

PREFACE

In this book I use the word fourth dimension in loose terms to make a point. The point being that God operates in a dimension outside of our reality, but can and does operate in our dimension at will.

The fourth dimension I see as an unseen realm that has substance, place, and purpose. It is heaven, space, time, and dimensional without end and beginning. God is its life and its power and its purpose.

In order for mankind to operate in the fourth dimension one must be transformed and changed. It is then that the born-again human can have the power and capacity to function as Jesus did.

1

DIMENSIONS

Think for a moment of living in a world that had no depth but only width and length. You wouldn't be able to comprehend distance, be limited in scope, range, without volume, and without the possibility of understanding character. This is the world of two dimensions; encompassing only one way of thinking, void of color, purpose, and imagination.

This way of thinking was the norm for the ancient thinkers. We can see in the scriptures the world of two dimensional thinking. It took God at His word, but failed to realize its depth and its power to transport the thinker into a world that demanded touch, power, presence, change, and action.

The New Testament in Jesus shed light on the God of depth, three dimensional realities, and focused purpose to add flesh to what was described for change and functioning power that the scriptures addressed and described.

When the old thinkers of the two dimensional word of God inheritors heard that the Word became flesh and dwelt amongst mankind it shook their world and made them angry[1]. After all, they thought, how could the two dimensional word they read and heard become flesh as it had no depth or substance? It was only an idea and often without the ability to do much more than to make one feel guilt of never living its demands or structure!

But, when Jesus showed up in the scope of man's two dimensional reality and declared that the

---

[1] John 1:1 In the beginning was the Word, and the Word was with God, and the Word was God. 2 He was in the beginning with God. NKJV

Word was more than written and had substance, power, and capable of living in a three dimensional world it brought forced change. The change demanded function and gravity to the extent that it pulled one to action.

God's presence in the earth through the Son brought out of the pages of the Torah a living and breathing three dimensional being that showed mankind how to make life work.

Even today, centuries beyond the creation's first days and the giving of the Word of God, mankind still finds it difficult to move past the two dimensions of the written word of God and make it functional in a three dimensional world. Most Christians are still dealing with a mindset of two dimensions.

Let me illustrate what I am describing. **Take for example the curtain in the temple of God on earth[2] thousands of years ago. On the curtain (veil) were two dimensional embroidered**

I.   [2] Heb 9:3 and behind the second veil, the part of the tabernacle which is called the Holiest of All, 4 which had the golden censer and the ark of the covenant overlaid on all sides with gold, in which were the golden pot that had the manna, Aaron's rod that budded, and the tablets of the covenant; 5 and above it were the cherubim of glory overshadowing the mercy seat. Of these things we cannot now speak in detail. NKJV cherubim. **When one entered behind the veil and saw the Ark of the Covenant one would see three dimensional representations of which the two dimensional embroidered cherubim represented on the front of the veil. So, one has to get past the two dimensional representations to realize the three dimensional realities. A change of place and a change of perspective really brings the change that is needed.**

Now, in all fairness, I know that most everyone would know that the embroidered cherubim represented the real thing. But, most never really had an encounter with real cherubim that would have changed their life.

The thing that would be needed in the case of the veil would be for a person to move from in front of the veil to behind the veil and see the three dimensional cherubim. There has to be change!

There has to be a change in order for a person to function outside of the normal Christian experience. That change which would cause one to move past two dimensional Christianity and into other dimensions in which we all were predestined to realize.

One of the most important tools given to us to realize greater spiritual dimension is God's word.

However, two dimensional Christianity only believes the word of God without experiencing the life that is in the word.

God's word is living, a two edged sword, life, food, a lamp, and capable of metamorphosing us to a place and reality that here-to-fore we have not experienced.

But, if one only sees the word of God in black and white terms but never permits it to change and transform, it will never move the believer into dimensions that glorify God and changes one's environment.

Two dimensional Christianity can't depart from the black and white of the written word of the Bible and into the functional reality of its truths. It lays dormant in the story, being infatuated by its tale or enamored by its beauty but never grasping its direction to be that which its life's conveyance depicts. It stays flat, without color, no power, and refuses to believe there is more to it than believing a truth only for the inner person. Two dimensional Christianity never sees three dimensional realities because it never moves to the place of action which causes one to touch, feel, experience, and engage. It is only for the future, in the by-and-by, but never for the here-and-now.

Two dimensional Christianity only sees the embroidered cherubims on a curtain which are pretty and glimmer of gold and only depict their three dimensional reality on the other side of the veil.

One must get past the black and white of the word of God and into living flesh of its power and changing abilities. After all, the word became flesh; Jesus being the word which became flesh. Becoming flesh makes the word of God animate[3]. Therefore those who are born of the word of God should have life and function in that which empowers their beliefs and actions. This leaves two dimensional Christianity in the dustbin of doubt.

If and when someone is truly born-again (the new creation) they are in a position to venture around the veil and see the cherubim in their three dimensional form on the mercy seat and realize their true beauty. This then is where each child of God must get to; around the veil of the two dimensional Christianity and into the realm where God's word is taken off of the black and white page and given form, function, and life.

---

[3] Animate: to impart life 2 to give spirit and vigor 3 to make appear to move.

The two different dimensions are separated by one thing, a curtain (veil) of unbelief which separates one dimension from the other; but if never entered into, a person never realizes the glory that is waiting for the adventurer. **Sadly, many Christians never go behind the veil and all they live and realize is a two dimensional spiritual world.**

But, God desires for us to live in a three dimensional reality that has the ability to bring us into a fourth dimension that transcends the reality of this world and makes us fit for greater things than we are earthly accustomed to. **We must make ourselves see past the immediate and the restricted realities of this world and into the possibilities of the spirit realm in which the born-again child of God lives.**

Once the "new creation" purposely believes and accepts reality and their new state of existence they are in a position to operate in the fourth dimension of the kingdom of God. It is that dimension which God desires, demands, and will empower those who take it seriously and practice its life producing tenets.

Jesus made it possible for us to live above and beyond this world's restrictions and move in His realm of victory[4]. It is in His realm of the dimension of kingdom living that we realize purity, power, and productivity[5].

Remember, when one is born-again one is something new, with new capabilities and new powers, with the capacity to live and function in the holy places with God. **We must truly comprehend the capacities we have for greater things, greater living, and great triumphs.**

Too often the born-again being lives way below their new capacities to affect their environment and ends up just being tossed to and fro by the whims of the world, the flesh, and the devil.

If we never realize or seek out the greater dimension of the Spirit we never experience or

---

[4] Heb 10:19 Therefore, brethren, having boldness to enter the Holiest by the blood of Jesus, 20 by a new and living way which He consecrated for us, through the veil, that is, His flesh, NKJV

[5] Matt 28:18 And Jesus came and spoke to them, saying, "All authority has been given to Me in heaven and on earth. 19 Go therefore and make disciples of all the nations, baptizing them in the name of the Father and of the Son and of the Holy Spirit, 20 teaching them to observe all things that I have commanded you; and lo, I am with you always, even to the end of the age." Amen. NKJV

partake of the deeper realities that God's children are ordained to function in.

Therefore, it is imperative that we never give ourselves the false luxury of sitting back and just making do until we die and go to heaven. We must comprehend the realities that are behind the veil and the deeper places of God's presence[6].

We must never give permission to doubt and lethargy to make us inept or a follower of the mindless weakness of fear, laziness, doubt, and incompetence. **There is too much at stake and too much to gain by not going behind the veil and working in the supernatural.**

Jesus gave us power and authority to move in the realm of the spirit and the ability to affect and

---

[6] **Col 2:20 Therefore, if you died with Christ from the basic principles of the world, why, as though living in the world, do you subject yourselves to regulations — 21 "Do not touch, do not taste, do not handle," 22 which all concern things which perish with the using — according to the commandments and doctrines of men? 23 These things indeed have an appearance of wisdom in self-imposed religion, false humility, and neglect of the body, but are of no value against the indulgence of the flesh. 3 If then you were raised with Christ, seek those things which are above, where Christ is, sitting at the right hand of God. 2 Set your mind on things above, not on things on the earth. 3 For you died, and your life is hidden with Christ in God. 4 When Christ who is our life appears, then you also will appear with Him in glory. NKJV**

change our environment. **That environment starts with your direct world, the place you live and the abilities you have. Then you take the environment in which you now live and have your being and affect everyone and everything around you.**

We must always keep this in mind, there is nothing we can't change, touch, and improve as we operate in the realm of God. We were born-again to do it!

Remember, it is in the third and fourth dimensions that things get done, and those who have entered into the fourth dimension of the Spirit of God get it done. **Col 2:20 Therefore, if you died with Christ from the basic principles of the world, why, as though living in the world, do you subject yourselves to regulations — 21 "Do not touch, do not taste, do not handle," 22 which all concern things which perish with the using — according to the commandments and doctrines of men? 23 These things indeed have an appearance of wisdom in self-imposed religion, false humility, and neglect of the body, but are of no value against the indulgence of the flesh. 3 If then you were raised with Christ, seek those things which are above, where Christ is, sitting at the right hand of God. 2 Set your mind on things above, not on things on the earth. 3 For** you died, and your life is hidden with Christ in God. 4 When Christ who is our life appears, then you also will appear with Him in glory. NKJV

2

SAVED FROM WHAT?

As we read what scripture tells us about salvation we can understand the full ramifications of what salvation is all about! As "new creations" we must fully understand what we are saved from and saved to. As you read the following scripture verses meditate on their full depth and ramification for those who call themselves 'saved'.

Isa 12:1 And in that day you will say: "O Lord I will praise You; Though You were angry with me, Your anger is turned away, and You comfort me. 2 Behold, God is my salvation, I will trust and not be afraid; 'For Yah, the Lord, is my strength and song; He also has become my salvation.'" 3 *Therefore with joy you will draw water From the wells of salvation.* 4 And in that day you will say: "Praise the Lord call upon His name; Declare His deeds among the peoples, Make mention that His name is exalted. NKJV

Matt 1:21 And she will bring forth a Son, and you shall call His name Jesus Jesus, for He will *save His people from their sins.*" NKJV

Luke 1:67 Now his father Zacharias was filled with the Holy Spirit, and prophesied, saying: 68 "Blessed is the Lord God of Israel, For He has visited and redeemed His people, 69 And has raised up a horn of salvation for us In the house of His servant David, 70 As He spoke by the mouth of His holy prophets, Who have been since the world began, 71 *That we should be saved from our enemies And from the hand of all who hate us,* NKJV

Rom 5:8-11 But God demonstrates His own love toward us, in that while we were still sinners, Christ died for us. 9 Much more then, having now been justified by His blood, _we shall be saved from wrath through Him_. 10 For if when we were enemies we were reconciled to God through the death of His Son, much more, having been reconciled, we shall be saved by His life. 11 And not only that, but we also rejoice in God through our Lord Jesus Christ, through whom we have now received the reconciliation. NKJV

What does it mean to be saved; what are we saved from and what are we saved to? **Knowing the answer to those questions insures that we truly understand and then walk in the fullness of what we are and have in God.**

God's plan for us includes much more than we often understand or give credit to. We need to grasp the full realization of our salvation.

When someone is saved from a disastrous situation we say they were saved. Let's say they were saved from a fire. But what are they saved from?

First, they were saved from death, hurt, pain, or some other terrible consequence of the moment. **When we are saved by our surrender to Jesus' sacrifice we are saved from the punishment of sins consequence; the separation from eternity**

15

with God and heaven's glory. Therefore it is paramount that you have received Jesus' gift of being your 'stand in' for your sins.

✓ We are saved from the enemy of sin. **Ps 18:3 I will call upon the Lord, who is worthy to be praised; So shall I be saved from my enemies. NKJV**

✓ We are saved from this perverse generation and the ramifications of being like it. **Acts 2:40 And with many other words he testified and exhorted them, saying, "Be saved from this perverse generation." 41 Then those who gladly received his word were baptized; and that day about three thousand souls were added to them. NKJV**

Second, they were saved from death, hurt, or pain to continue on in life and brought back to the state of living as before; but with spiritual salvation there is a caveat (a warning). **The caveat or warning stipulates that you cannot go on living as before, there must be a change!**

✓ The first change makes us someone different by an outward transformation and an inward metamorphoses.

• **The outward gives us the robe of righteousness that must be fitted through use.**

• **The inward metamorphoses only happens as we make choices**

to be the person God has ordained His children to be; people holy, righteous, and pure.

✓ People are saved in order to become someone and something different than their former state and situation and brought into something totally new with the primary goal and endeavor to bring glory to the One who made them – God. They become a "New Creation!"

The new "Saved" status makes a person totally different, having the same earthly qualities but the capacity of heaven's reality.

Jesus doesn't take us out of the world after we are saved, He transforms us so that we are capable of doing what He did to change the world, by using supernatural abilities to affect our environment. **John 17:13 But now I come to You, and these things I speak in the world, that they may have My joy fulfilled in themselves. 14 I have given them Your word; and the world has hated them because they are not of the world, just as I am not of the world. 15 I do not pray that You should take them out of the world, but that You should keep them from the evil one. 16 They are not of the world, just as I am not of the world. 17 Sanctify them by Your truth. Your** word is truth. 18 As You sent Me into the world, I also have sent them into the world. 19 And for their sakes I sanctify Myself, that they also may be sanctified by the truth. 20 "I do not pray for these alone, but also for those who will believe in Me through their word; 21 that they all may be one, as You, Father, are in Me, and I in You; that they also may be one in Us, that the world may believe that You sent Me. 22 And the glory which You gave Me I have given them, that they may be one just as We are one: 23 I in them, and You in Me; that they may be made perfect in one, and that the world may know that You have sent Me, and have loved them as You have loved Me. NKJV

The first thing we have access to is 'joy'. **If you refuse or do not practice joy it is your own fault for unhappiness, frustrations, and heaviness.**

Second, we have been sanctified by God's truth. **God's truth can only be found in His word and it is our food and sustenance for this earthly living.**

Third, we are not only with one another, because we are of the family of believers, but we are one with the Father and the Son. **It is important that we have a sense of family; one with each** other and practice that concept and then realize we really are one with the Father, Son, and Spirit.

Fourth, we have the protection of the Father from the evil one – Satan. **Never, but never, let the enemy, by whatever means, convince you that you can't win over him in any situation. You are truly under the Father's protection and more than a conqueror through Jesus**

3

ONE WITH HIM

Lev 16:21 Aaron shall lay both his hands on the head of the live goat, confess over it all the iniquities of the children of Israel, and all their transgressions, concerning all their sins, putting them on the head of the goat, and shall send it away into the wilderness by the hand of a suitable man. 22 The goat shall bear on itself all their iniquities to an uninhabited land; and he shall release the goat in the wilderness. NKJV

Gal 2:20 I have been crucified with Christ; it is no longer I who live, but Christ lives in me; and the life which I now live in the flesh I live by

faith in the Son of God, who loved me and gave Himself for me. NKJV

1 Peter 5:6 Therefore humble yourselves under the mighty hand of God, that He may exalt you in due time, **7** casting all your care upon Him, for He cares for you. **NKJV**

1 John 1:8 If we say that we have no sin, we deceive ourselves, and the truth is not in us. **9** If we confess our sins, He is faithful and just to forgive us our sins and to cleanse us from all unrighteousness. **NKJV**

One of the mysteries of being a blood bought child of God and becoming a New Creation is the fact that you must become one with Jesus' sacrifice for your sins.

It isn't enough just to confess our sins, we must totally engage in the process that separates our life from those sins and the effects they caused. **What Jesus did for us He did by the transference of our sins by our declaration of our guilt upon Him through our will!** The Hebrews did this through the Priest performing the '*Semikhah*'. (*Each person would take their offering sacrifice to the Priest, lay their hands on its head and pronounce their sins over the animal and then the* *animal would be killed or sent out into the wilderness for the forgiveness of the sins.)*

But how do we do this today when Jesus died only once thousands of years ago? **We do this by really comprehending the dreadfulness of our sins and the reality of Jesus's life, death, and resurrection for us.**

First, do we really understand the dreadfulness of our sins and how it affects God? We must know what sin does!

- Sin makes us unfit for heavenly living and eternal productivity. **Heaven demands perfection but sin contaminates and corrupts; therefore one must be cleansed of its corruption in order to enjoy and partake of heavens beauty.** Jesus' sacrifice removes the corruption.
- Sin affects God by making Him turn away from anything that is not Holy, righteous, and pure; it cannot be in His presence because He is totally pure and perfect.

Second, we must really believe, comprehend, accept, and be one with Jesus's sacrifice.

- It isn't enough just to repeat words, make announcements one may not understand, or go along with someone else's understanding; we must know it for ourselves to the best of our ability. **Do you personally believe Jesus lived, died for 'your' sins and was resurrected?**
- To know and believe this truth must come from a felt reality about one's own sins and an understanding that someone else has to make it right for us because we can't do it; that someone else is Jesus!

Our becoming one with our sacrifice, Jesus being that sacrifice, puts us in a place of humility and an understanding of our weakness and low estate of life without God's help. **It is always good for us to remember that we cannot do anything perfect, pure, and good without God's direct intervention as we surrender to His input.**

The moment or moments we can perform our Semikhah (placing our sins/, problems, and shortcomings) on Jesus' head and become one with His life, His suffering, His resurrection is the time/s that we find release and become truly one with Him.

That is what it is all about, being one with Him, one with the Father, and one with His Spirit who directs our lives.

It is only through a life that surrenders and wants a true oneness with God that we find peace, joy, and contentment in this world.

These surrendering moments can come to us as we just let go and let God take it all, fill us with Himself, and completely engulf us with His presence.

We must learn to rest in God's reality and His person. **Really know He is real, He is with you now, and He wants an interaction of life with you!**

Don't just be saved, be one with God; enjoy His life and His forgiveness and His ongoing History with you. **Learn to have a history with God, not just a thought that God is, but have a way of life with Him.**

4

WHAT IS OUR PURPOSE?

**Acts 9:5 And he said, "Who are You, Lord?"
Then the Lord said, "I am Jesus, whom you are
persecuting. It is hard for you to kick against the
goads." NKJV**

Saul didn't know Jesus, but he was fighting
what God wanted to do in the earth and for the
Jews. Often we fight against God because we are
ignorant to His purposes and goals for us. We need
to stop, take stock of what life is really about, and
be sensitive to what God may be doing and wants us
to do in life. After all, we are now new creations

and it makes sense that we find out what our purpose is.

2 Tim 1:8 Therefore do not be ashamed of the testimony of our Lord, nor of me His prisoner, but share with me in the sufferings for the gospel according to the power of God, 9 who has saved us and called us with a holy calling, not according to our works, _but according to His own purpose and grace_ which was given to us in Christ Jesus before time began, NKJV

God has a purpose for each of us and by His grace it will work out and we need to realize what it is.

1 John 5:18 We know that whoever is born of God does not sin; but he who has been born of God keeps himself, and the wicked one does not touch him. 19 We know that we are of God, and the whole world lies under the sway of the wicked one. 20 And we know that the Son of God has come and has given us an understanding, that we may know Him who is true; and we are in Him who is true, in His Son Jesus Christ. This is the true God and eternal life. NKJV

If the truth of our existence is to know Him who is true, we must constantly seek out His life,

His ways of doing life, and His power to bring forth and accomplish our destiny.

Phil 3:7 But what things were gain to me, these I have counted loss for Christ. 8 Yet indeed I also count all things loss for the excellence of the knowledge of Christ Jesus my Lord, for whom I have suffered the loss of all things, and count them as rubbish, that I may gain Christ 9 and be found in Him, not having my own righteousness, which is from the law, but that which is through faith in Christ, the righteousness which is from God by faith; 10 that I may know Him *and the power of His resurrection*, and the fellowship of His sufferings, being conformed to His death, 11 if, by any means, I may attain to the resurrection from the dead. NKJV

Too often most Christians do not know the power of His resurrection because all they do is keep on seeking their old familiar ways and life style of this world instead of gaining knowledge and understanding their new capabilities of the new creation.

Phil 3:12 Not that I have already attained, or am already perfected; but I press on, that I may lay hold of that for which Christ Jesus has also laid

hold of me. 13 Brethren, I do not count myself to have apprehended; but one thing I do, forgetting those things which are behind and reaching forward to those things which are ahead, 14 I press toward the goal for the prize of the upward call of God in Christ Jesus. 15 Therefore let us, as many as are mature, have this mind; and if in anything you think otherwise, God will reveal even this to you. 16 Nevertheless, to the degree that we have already attained, let us walk by the same rule, let us be of the same mind. NKJV

What are the things ahead? What is the goal? What is the upward call? What is the rule we are to walk by?

- ✓ The things ahead are new powers to live godly, new abilities that all too often lay dormant but have been given to us by God and activated by the new birth.
- ✓ The goal is to know and work with and operate with God as He lives through us and out of us.
- ✓ The upward call is to take everything in your life and in this life and make it like that of heaven. Not leaving anything of this world untouched by your new creation powers for change.
- ✓ The rule we are to walk by is the rule of love and grace. A new creation person has at their disposal the most powerful

fourth dimension weapon there is, love that overcomes and faith that moves fleshy obstacles.

Always remember, we each have a beginning and an end, what we do in the in-between of those two makes all the difference when everything is said and done.

We aren't saved and born-again to sit and do nothing; we are to work at this righteous life and move toward knowing God more and working with Him constantly. **Heb 12:2 looking unto Jesus, the author and finisher of our faith, who for the joy that was set before Him endured the cross, despising the shame, and has sat down at the right hand of the throne of God. NKJV**

There is a lot of living to do between the authorship of Jesus stamped on our life and our faith to the finishing of our existence with Him on this planet.

Too often many get "saved" and just continue on without much change, but for those who are born-again life must be mastered through the Holy Spirit's power and made effective in the doing and known purposes of God.

The known purposes of God come through love, power, and a sound mind. **2 Tim 1:7 For God has not given us a spirit of fear, but of power and of love and of a sound mind. NKJV**

We then must permit the Holy Spirit to quicken us daily to bring about the purposes of God in and through us.

5

THE NEW CREATION,

A CONTAINER OF GOD

John 3:1 There was a man of the Pharisees named Nicodemus, a ruler of the Jews. 2 This man came to Jesus by night and said to Him, "Rabbi, we know that You are a teacher come from God; for no one can do these signs that You do unless God is with him." 3 Jesus answered and said to him, "Most assuredly, I say to you, unless one is born again, he cannot see the kingdom of God." 4 Nicodemus said to Him, "How can a man be born when he is old? Can he enter a second time into his mother's womb and be born?" 5 Jesus answered, "Most assuredly, I say to you, unless one is born of water and the Spirit, he cannot enter the kingdom of God. 6 That which is born of the flesh is flesh, and that which is born of the Spirit is spirit. 7 Do not marvel that I said to you, 'You must be born again.' 8 The wind blows where it wishes, and you hear the sound of it, but cannot tell where it comes from and where it goes. So is everyone who is born of the Spirit." NKJV

Jesus was ensuring that Nicodemus understood that he had to be born-again into the spirit of heaven and made a new creation.

2 Cor 5:16 Therefore, from now on, we regard no one according to the flesh. Even though we have known Christ according to the flesh, yet now we know Him thus no longer. 17 Therefore, if anyone is in Christ, he is a new creation; old things have passed away; behold, all things have become new. NKJV

The only way you can know spiritual things is by being born in the spirit.

l 6:14-15 But God forbid that I should boast except in the cross of our Lord Jesus Christ, by whom the world has been crucified to me, and I to the world. **15 For in Christ Jesus neither circumcision nor uncircumcision avails anything, but a new creation. NKJV**

The most important thing that matters and is powerful is someone who is a new creation filled with the Holy Spirit.

Acts 1:6-8 Therefore, when they had come together, they asked Him, saying, "Lord, will You at this time restore the kingdom to Israel?" 7 And He said to them, "It is not for you to know times or seasons which the Father has put in His own authority. 8 But you shall receive power when the Holy Spirit has come upon you; and you shall be witnesses to Me in Jerusalem, and in all Judea and Samaria, and to the end of the earth." NKJV

It was most important for Jesus to ensure they knew that they must receive the power of the Holy Spirit in order for them to live a life of power in this earth.

Acts 8:14 Now when the apostles who were at Jerusalem heard that Samaria had received the word of God, they sent Peter and John to them, 15 who, when they had come down, prayed for them that they might receive the Holy Spirit. 16

For as yet He had fallen upon none of them. They had only been baptized in the name of the Lord Jesus. 17 Then they laid hands on them, and they received the Holy Spirit. NKJV

This gives evidence that being baptized in the Holy Spirit can be a separate and distinct experience.

Acts 10:44 While Peter was still speaking these words, the Holy Spirit fell upon all those who heard the word. 45 And those of the circumcision who believed were astonished, as many as came with Peter, because the gift of the Holy Spirit had been poured out on the Gentiles also. 46 _For they heard them speak with tongues and magnify God_. Then Peter answered, 47 "Can anyone forbid water, that these should not be baptized who have received the Holy Spirit just as we have?" 48 And he commanded them to be baptized in the name of the Lord. Then they asked him to stay a few days. NKJV

Even though they received the Holy Spirit they still needed to be baptized in Jesus' name to confirm their surrender and allegiance to God.

Acts 19:1 And it happened, while Apollos was at Corinth, that Paul, having passed through the upper regions, came to Ephesus. And finding

some disciples 2 he said to them, "Did you receive the Holy Spirit when you believed?" So they said to him, "We have not so much as heard whether there is a Holy Spirit." 3 And he said to them, "Into what then were you baptized?" So they said, "Into John's baptism." 4 Then Paul said, "John indeed baptized with a baptism of repentance, saying to the people that they should believe on Him who would come after him, that is, on Christ Jesus." (John's baptism was a baptism for repentance of sin and looking to the Messiah to come – Jesus.) 5 When they heard this, they were baptized in the name of the Lord Jesus. 6 _**And when Paul had laid hands on them, the Holy Spirit came upon them, and they spoke with tongues and prophesied.**_ 7 Now the men were about twelve in all. NKJV

Once we understand the above information we can comprehend the reality of what the born-again person is; we are recipients and containers of the Holy Spirit. **Yes, the very home, temple, and residence of the Holy Spirit.**

It is imperative that we seek out the same reality as those of the early church. Surrendering to Jesus and desiring the empowerment of the Holy Spirit must never be denied or forgotten about in one's quest for holiness and righteousness.

It is important that we permit the Holy Spirit to totally empower and engulf us.

It is not enough to be saved without power. **Remember, salvation is being saved for something as well as being saved from something.**

When the Holy Spirit baptizes us He empowers us to live for God and walk in spiritual abilities and powers that we did not understand nor seek out before He comes upon us.

We are not born-again and saved just to be happy and free, we are born-again to do for God and walk in power.

Being baptized in the Holy Spirit makes us the totally new creation being that God intended for us to be, whereas before the baptism of the Holy Spirit we are just human beings who believe in God. **I do not make light of this, but surely God wants more than just believers who do nothing.**

It is just for that reason that we must not only be born-again but also baptized in the Holy Spirit!

We must surrender to God's way of the new creation life. Asking and seeking to be empowered by the Holy Spirit, and knowingly and willingly walking in spiritual realities and power.

We must purposely move away from the existence we were first born into and then seek out and willfully work the new life of the Holy Spirit. **I think it is imperative that we purposely transform our thinking from the restrictions of the earthly existence and begin to move in the supernatural. That begins by being baptized in the Holy Spirit.**

It all has to do with surrender! You can have it if you desire it.

You must be born-again and filled with the Holy Spirit! In this way one moves and operates in the fourth dimension.

6

THE FOURTH DIMENSION

If a person would try to imagine life from God's perspective I'm sure one would realize a totally different existence.

The ancients had no idea of earth in all of its complexities and place in the solar system. Their only perspective came from their feet planted on this planet without the advantage from an observation from space. But we in the twenty first century have the advantage of satellites, airplanes, and spacecrafts. Our perspective informs us of what is possible as twenty first century inhabitants. We know what we can do with the technology and the wherewithal we have been given and have access to. We can and do things that Adam and Eve had no idea of.

Adam and Eve had no idea of what they could have done because they never got to the point of realizing their full potential because of sin and disobedience. Their perspective was limited to earth's laws of physics and the like which govern those who are only built for two and three dimensional realities. But God wanted more for His children and fashioned mankind to live in another dimension governed by spiritual laws that encompasses much more.

Scripture is full of examples, peppered with true accounts, and lived out adventures of what was possible for those who would believe and be touched by a dimension different than the ones they were accustomed to.

It's the fourth dimension that is only visible from the other side of our reality. It is all around us, just out of reach, very much real, and totally capable of being mastered by anyone who would be changed.

It's the dimension that Jesus walked in. It is the place that heaven operates in and the laws that govern the kingdom of God.

Jesus, being the Son of God who came from heaven and God's presence, has/had His being in the dimension I call the fourth dimension.

That dimension governs everything in the known universe and all of existence and before created time and space. It is a dimension that God in His wisdom created mankind to live in after testing.

Because of the disobedience of Adam, mankind would never have had the opportunity to realize God's plan for four dimensional living. Jesus knows/knew it and some were touched by it in scripture. But God wants everyone to operate in it. What is needed is change!

Let's look at those who were given access to the fourth dimension in scripture; those who for brief moments operated in a dimension that was perplexing but inspiring, that in many cases lasted the rest of their lives.

Obviously, Jesus was the first human that operated in the fourth dimension on earth.

We know that Jesus was filled with the Holy Spirit even before His birth. But, we must never forget the fact that before His baptism by John the

43

Baptist he did not move in the supernatural. At least we do not have any scriptural evidence.

Needless to say, after Jesus' baptism and the Holy Spirit coming upon Him, we see Him operating in the power of the Holy Spirit and affecting the third dimension and His environment.

It seemed that casting out demons, healing the sick, and raising the dead was as easy as breathing to Jesus. The power He displayed came from a source and place outside of the norm, but by His own admission was very much in reach of all. Belief and change was all that was needed!

Trying to get the disciples to understand the power of God was one of Jesus' major themes. He would say that it was easier to say than to do. He would instruct by example and showed annoyance when the disciples wouldn't get it.

The lesson for me in those encounters makes me want to cast off the plague of doubt that tries to dissuade me.

Disciples

After Jesus was taken up into heaven the disciples went to Jerusalem and waited for the promise of the Holy Spirit of which He told them about. On the day of Pentecost the disciples were baptized in the Holy Spirit and power[7].

The original one hundred and twenty disciples were the first of those who had believed in Jesus and His changing power.

After the initial empowerment of the Holy Spirit on those first disciples we see a drastic change in their lives. Whereas before the moment of the outpouring of the Holy Spirit the disciples were afraid and feared for their lives, they now were fearless and doing miraculous deeds. In an essence they were born-again and made New Creations.

Those disciples new creation experience put them in the realm of the fourth dimension and capable of doing the same things Jesus did while on earth.

Those disciples were now functioning in a dimension that had power over their familiar environment and its limitations and weaknesses.

---

[7] Acts 2:1 When the day of Pentecost came, they were all together in one place. 2 Suddenly a sound like the blowing of a violent wind came from heaven and filled the whole house where they were sitting. 3 They saw what seemed to be tongues of fire that separated and came to rest on each of them. 4 All of them were filled with the Holy Spirit and began to speak in other tongues as the Spirit enabled them. NIV

The born-again, New Creation reality put them in a position to use the tools and resources of heaven. It was the very power He used and expected His disciples to use to further the kingdom of God.

We see Peter's shadow falling on people and they are healed. We read of Phillip being transported to a new location. Paul's life changing conversion and raising people from the dead demonstrates what fourth dimension reality is all about for those who are changed.

The New Creation change caused all of the many miracles that were performed by the apostles (Acts 2:43). Peter healed the lame man at the Temple (Acts 3:7-11). God answered Peter in a miraculous earthquake (Acts 4:31). Signs and wonders continued to be done by the apostles (Acts 5:12). Peter healed many from various cities (Acts 5:12-16). The prison doors were opened by an angel (Acts 5:19). Stephen wrought great wonders and signs (Acts 6:8). In Samaria, Philip did great miracles and signs (Acts 8:6,7,13).

Ananias healed Saul's blindness (Acts 9:17-18). Peter healed Aeneas (Acts 9:32-35). In Joppa, Peter raised Dorcus from the dead (Acts 9:39-42).

Cornelius saw an angel. He and his family spoke in tongues, but he was saved by responding to the preaching of the gospel by Peter (Acts 10:4,46;

cf. v. 48; 11:14). Peter saw the vision on the roof and spoke with the Lord (Acts 10:9-22).

A prison gate was miraculously opened (Acts 12:10). Paul blinded Elymus (Acts 13:11-12). Paul performed miracles in Iconium (Acts 14:3,4). At Lystra, Paul healed a crippled man (Acts 14:8-18). Paul healed a woman possessed by an evil spirit (Acts 16:18). The miraculous earthquake unloosed all the chains and doors in the Philippian prison (Acts 16:26). In Ephesus, twelve men spoke in tongues, and prophesied (Acts 19:6). Paul performed other miracles in Ephesus (Acts 19:11,12). In Troas, Paul raised Eutychus from the dead (Acts 20:8-12). Paul was not affected by the viper at Melita (Acts 28:3-6). He also healed those on the island who were diseased (Acts 28:8-9).

As we can see, if one were to "demythologize" the book of Acts, as those of a liberal bent try to do, much would be missing concerning the amazing growth and development of the early church. In fact, we would have a difficult time explaining how so many Greeks, Romans, and "barbarians" (i.e., non-Greeks), obeyed the gospel. Is it rational to think that Paul is going to walk onto some island in the Mediterranean and convert many people simply because he is convincing, or friendly —or was there some other reason? To the contrary, they observed indisputable deeds that confirmed the message of the apostle. In case after case, many believed the message that was confirmed by the miracles. This is one reason for the amazing success that the gospel enjoyed in the first century.

All of those miracles give the most convincing proof of the reality and power of those who operate from the fourth dimension. It must be one of the most convincing arguments for those who are born-again, believe in faith, and are baptized in the Holy Spirit. They all become fourth dimensional citizens with ability to function in the supernatural. After all, the supernatural does not have its origin from earth and the third dimension but from the fourth dimension of heaven.

It is from heavens operation that those who are made New Creations can function and overcome third dimensions restrictions.

Old Testament

Ezek 36:24 For I will take you from among the nations, gather you out of all countries, and bring you into your own land. 25 Then I will sprinkle clean water on you, and you shall be clean; I will cleanse you from all your filthiness and from all your idols. 26 I will give you a new heart and put a new spirit within you;

I will take the heart of stone out of your flesh and give you a heart of flesh. 27 I will put My Spirit within you and cause you to walk in My statutes, and you will keep My judgments and do them. NKJV

The above verse is one of the first verses in the Old Testament in which God tells Israel what His hearts intention for them is. He desired for every one of His people to be filled with His Spirit which would give them power to be everything He intended for all.

There will come a time after Israel has been brought back to the land of promise that every one of God's people will be filled with His Spirit and they will live the truth. It will be a national transformation that the world has not yet realized in mass.

The filling, in part for those who would believe in the Messiah, did take place on the day of Pentecost after Jesus had ascended to heaven, but as a whole, this filling is in the future.

However, there are others in the Old Testament like Moses who were filled with God's Spirit and moved in His power.

After Moses had his experience with the burning bush and God's calling him to lead His people from Egypt, God filled Moses with His Spirit.

From that moment on Moses did extraordinary exploits for God and revealed the power of God's Spirit to the masses.

Moses was changed by the encounter at the burning bush and opened his life to God's abilities through him. It is one of those graphic examples that demonstrate that one's life must have a transforming moment for God to be able to empower and for His Spirit to reside in His created beings.

But, it should be noted that the encounters and changes for those in the Old Testament for the most part were not the norm, but the exception.

However, as we have seen from the historical biblical record, that those who are born-again, filled with the Holy Spirit and made New Creations are capable of functioning from the fourth dimension.

www.ingramcontent.com/pod-product-compliance
Lightning Source LLC
Chambersburg PA
CBHW060611030426
42337CB00018B/3035